The Best of Our Lives

The Best
Of Our Lives

A Celebration of the Golden Years

Edited by Elmer S. Newman

Illustrated by Asterio Pascolini

♕ HALLMARK EDITIONS

For age is opportunity no less
Than youth itself, though in another dress,
And as the evening twilight fades away
The sky is filled with stars, invisible by day.
  — *Henry Wadsworth Longfellow*

On Being a Grandmother:
Mrs. Rose Kennedy

Recently, Mrs. Kennedy said it is not the passing of time which ages us, but the way we deal with life. Mrs. Kennedy still fills an important place in the Kennedy family life, as she shows here in describing her relationship with her twenty-eight grandchildren.

I keep *au courant* with what is going on in the world and in their worlds. They know that I think that from those to whom much has been given much is to be expected, as Luke said. There are no gaps as we are a cohesive family group, no deviousness. If I think criticism is necessary, I say so directly. That's when notes are handy. I learned that from my father. He pinned notes on himself.

At the table I put the older children together, letting the younger ones eat earlier. And we talk about national events, about what was in the morning paper or on the television news. We talked about the significance of certain religious holidays recently. Some of the children did not know about the Feast of Passover, did not know who was at the Cross when He died.

If the spread between the ages is too wide at

table, the older ones do all the talking and the smaller ones all the listening. The little ones have no chance.

On Sundays, however, when the smallest ones were old enough, we had all nine children together for dinner. After Kathleen Kennedy—my oldest granddaughter, the oldest child of Bobby and Ethel—had worked during one summer with the Eskimos in Alaska and the Indians in the West, we talked at dinner about the problems of those children, of helping others.

People sometimes feel sorry for me; God has given me many joys and sorrows. He intends us to be happy, intends us to have joy as well as heartache. So many people dwell on the past. Enjoy the present. I am reminded of these favorite lines of President Kennedy's in *Ecclesiastes:* "To everything there is a season, and a time to every purpose under the Heaven: ...A time to weep, and a time to laugh; a time to mourn, and a time to dance...."

Now, I am finding joy and happiness, enrichment and fulfillment in my life with my children and grandchildren.

What is important is how we rise to tragedies and heartaches and disappointments. That is what makes us valiant.

• • •

When a man achieves a fair measure of harmony within himself and his family circle, he achieves peace; and a nation made up of such individuals and groups is a happy nation. As the harmony of a star in its course is expressed by rhythm and grace, so the harmony of a man's life-course is expressed by happiness; this, I believe, is the prime desire of mankind.

— *Richard E. Byrd*

More are men's ends mark'd than their
lives before:
  The setting sun, and music at the close,
As the last taste of sweets, is sweetest last,
Writ in remembrance more than things
long past.

— *William Shakespeare*

When you dig another out of his trouble, you find a place to bury your own.

— *Author unknown*

Each part of life has its own abundant harvest, to be garnered in season. Old age is rich in blessings.

— *Cicero*

There is youth in me, in most of us, who would be carefree and happy, "bird happy," and would find it natural and enough. Knowing that destruction and creation are twin brothers, that the gods destroy and create — why else are they called gods? — I hear without surprise someone in me saying: "But life is delicious, what beauty, what interest, I wouldn't have missed it for worlds. Look at the day, feel the air, you see for yourself, all is well."

— *Florida Scott-Maxwell*

May you live all the days of your life.
— *Jonathan Swift*

To be seventy years young is sometimes far more cheerful and hopeful than to be forty years old.

— *Oliver Wendell Holmes*

Spring still makes spring in the mind
   When sixty years are told;
Love wakes anew this throbbing heart,
   And we are never old;
Over the winter glaciers
   I see the summer glow,
And through the wild-piled snowdrift
   The warm rosebuds below.
         — *Ralph Waldo Emerson*

Remember the Model T?:
Lee Strout White

If "there's a Ford in your future," there very well may have been a Ford in your past... a Model T Ford. The nature of that unique machine and its typical owner are set out here in graphic detail.

There was this about a Model T: the purchaser never regarded his purchase as a complete, finished product. When you bought a Ford, you figured you had a start — a vibrant, spirited framework to which could be screwed an almost limitless assortment of decorative and functional hardware. Driving away from the agency, hugging the new wheel between your knees, you were already full of creative worry. A Ford was born naked as a baby, and a flourishing industry grew up out of correcting its rare deficiencies and combatting its fascinating diseases. Those were the great days of lily-painting. I have been looking at some old Sears Roebuck catalogues, and they bring everything back so clear.

First you bought a Ruby Safety Reflector for the rear, so that your posterior would glow in another car's brilliance. Then you invested thirty-nine cents in some radiator Moto

Wings, a popular ornament which gave the Pegasus touch to the machine and did something godlike to the owner. For nine cents you bought a fan-belt guide to keep the belt from slipping off the pulley.

You bought a radiator compound to stop leaks. This was as much a part of everybody's equipment as aspirin tablets are of a medicine cabinet. You bought special oil to prevent chattering, a clamp-on dash light, a patching outfit, a tool box which you bolted to the running board, a sun visor, a steering-column brace to keep the column rigid, and a set of emergency containers for gas, oil, and water — three thin, disc-like cans which reposed in a case on the running board during long, important journeys — red for gas, gray for water, green for oil. It was only a beginning. After the car was about a year old, steps were taken to check the alarming disintegration. (Model T was full of tumors, but they were benign.) A set of anti-rattlers (98¢) was a popular panacea. You hooked them on to the gas and spark rods, to the brake pull rod, and to the steering-rod connections. Hood silencers, of black rubber, were applied to the fluttering hood. Shock-absorbers and snubbers gave "complete relaxation." Some people bought rubber pedal pads, to fit over the standard metal pedals. (I didn't like these, I remember.) Persons of a suspicious or pugnacious turn of mind bought a rear-view mirror; but most Model T owners weren't worried by what was coming from behind because they would soon enough see it out in front. They rode in a state of cheerful catalepsy.

• • •

When I was young my teachers were the old.
I gave up fire for form till I was cold.
I suffered like a metal being cast.
I went to school to age to learn the past.

Now I am old my teachers are the young.
What can't be moulded must be cracked
    and sprung.
I strain at lessons fit to start a suture.
I go to school to youth to learn the future.
                              — *Robert Frost*

We do not count a man's years, until he has nothing else to count.
                              — *Ralph Waldo Emerson*

A New Life at Eighty: Grandma Moses

When she could no longer do needlework, Grandma Moses, nearing eighty, took up painting...and she soon achieved a national reputation. She died at age 101 and in the year before her death had completed twenty-five paintings.

As for myself, I started to paint in my old age, one might say, though I had painted a few pictures before. My sister Celestia came down one day and saw my worsted pictures and said: "I think you could paint better and faster than you could do worsted pictures." So I did, and painted for pleasure, to keep busy and to pass the time away, but I thought of it no more than of doing fancy work.

When I had quite a few paintings on hand, someone suggested that I send them down to the old Thomas' drug store in Hoosick Falls, so I tried that. I also exhibited a few at the Cambridge Fair with some canned fruits and raspberry jam. I won a prize for my fruit and jam, but no pictures.

And then, one day, a Mr. Louis J. Caldor of New York City, an engineer and art collector, passing through the town of Hoosick Falls, saw and bought my paintings. He wanted to know who had painted them, and they told him it was an old woman that was living down on the Cambridge Road by the name of Anna Mary Moses. So when I came home that night, Dorothy said: "If you had been here, you could have sold all your paintings, there was a man here looking for them, and he will be back in the morning to see them. I told him how many you had." She thought I had about ten, something like that.

Well, I didn't sleep much that night, I tried to think where I had any paintings and what they were, I knew I didn't have many, they were mostly worsted, but I thought, towards morning, of a painting I had started on after house cleaning days, when I found an old canvas and frame, and I thought I had painted a picture on it of Virginia. It was quite large, and I thought if I could find frames in the morning I could cut that right in two and make two pictures, which I did, and by so doing I had the ten pictures for him when he came. I did it so it wouldn't get Dorothy in the doghouse. But he didn't discover the one I had cut in two for about a year, then he wanted to know what made me cut my best picture in two. I told him, it's just Scotch thrift.

• • •

If a man does not make new acquaintances, as he advances through life, he will soon find himself left alone. A man should keep his friendship in constant repair.
— *Samuel Johnson*

My Heart Leaps Up

My heart leaps up when I behold
A rainbow in the sky:
So was it when my life began,
So is it now I am a man,
So be it when I shall grow old
Or let me die!
The Child is father of the Man:
And I could wish my days to be
Bound each to each by natural piety.
— *William Wordsworth*

Be a life long or short, its completeness depends on what it was lived for.
— *David Starr Jordan*

Look for a lovely thing and you will find it.
— *Sara Teasdale*

The Art of Growing Old: Bertrand Russell

Lord Russell knew a great deal about growing old and outliving one's friends. He lived to be ninety-seven. The essay from which this excerpt is taken was written as he approached his eightieth birthday.

The art of growing old is one which the passage of time has forced upon my attention. Psychologically there are two dangers to be guarded against in old age. One of these is undue absorption in the past. It does not do to live in memories, in regrets for the good old days....One's thoughts must be directed to the future, and to things about which there is something to be done. This is not always easy; one's own past is a gradually increasing weight. It is easy to think to oneself that one's emotions used to be more vivid than they are, and one's mind more keen. If this is true it should be forgotten, and if it is forgotten it will probably not be true.

The other thing to be avoided is clinging to youth in the hope of sucking vigor from its vitality. When your children are grown up they want to live their own lives, and if you continue to be as interested in them as you were when they were young, you are likely to become a burden to them, unless they are unusually callous. I do not mean that one should be without interest in them, but one's interest should be contemplative and, if possible, philanthropic, but not unduly emotional. Animals become indifferent to their young as soon as their young can look after themselves, but human beings, owing to the length of infancy, find this difficult.

I think that a successful old age is easiest for those who have strong impersonal interests involving appropriate activities. It is in this sphere that long experience is really fruitful, and it is in this sphere that the wisdom born of experience can be exercised without being oppressive.

• • •

Whether one is twenty, forty, sixty or eighty; whether one has succeeded, failed, or just muddled along — Life Begins Each Morning!

Life is a day — this day. All past days are gone beyond reviving. All days that still may come are veiled in mystery. Each new day is Life, and life begins anew with it.

— *L. M. Hodges*

I think you'll like this anecdote told to me by Warren Wire, of Los Angeles. "Last Christmas," he writes, "my daughter and son-in-law and their six-year-old Steven were among our guests. After dinner, we watched a football game on television, and that led to a general discussion of sports.

"One said he liked prize fights best; another golf; a third baseball. Somebody finally asked young Steven what kind of sport he liked best. He looked in turn at everybody in the room, then came over and threw his arms around me, and said, 'MY GRAN'PA.'"

— *Bennett Cerf*

Blessed is the man who can enjoy the small things, the common beauties, the little day-by-day events; sunshine on the fields, birds on the bough, breakfast, dinner, supper, the daily paper on the porch, a friend passing by. So many people who go afield for enjoyment leave it behind them at home.

— *David Grayson*

The Wonder of the World:
John Burroughs and Henry David Thoreau

John Burroughs, America's great naturalist expresses nature's grandeur and beauty.
The longer I live the more my mind dwells upon the beauty and the wonder of the world. I hardly know which feeling leads, wonderment or admiration. After a man has passed the psalmist's dead line of seventy years, as Dr. Holmes called it, if he is of a certain temperament, he becomes more and more detached from the noise and turmoil of the times in which he lives. The passing hubbub in the street attracts him less and less; more and more he turns to the permanent, the fundamental, the everlasting. More and more is he impressed with life and nature in themselves, and the beauty and the grandeur of the voyage we are making on this planet.

The splendor and wonderment is expressed in Henry David Thoreau's American classic, Walden.
The first sparrow of spring! The year beginning with younger hope than ever! The faint silvery warblings heard over the partially bare and moist fields from the bluebird, the

song-sparrow, and the red-wing, as if the last flakes of winter tinkled as they fell! What at such a time are histories, chronologies, traditions, and all written revelations? The brooks sing carols and glees to the spring. The marsh-hawk sailing low over the meadow is already seeking the first slimy life that awakes. The sinking sound of melting snow is heard in all dells, and the ice dissolves apace in the ponds. The grass flames up on the hillsides like a spring fire,...as if the earth sent forth an inward heat to greet the returning sun; not yellow but green is the color of its flame;—the symbol of perpetual youth, the grass-blade, like a long green ribbon, streams from the sod into the summer, checked indeed by the frost, but anon pushing on again, lifting its spear of last year's hay with the fresh life below. It grows as steadily as the rill oozes out of the ground. It is almost identical with that, for in the growing days of June, when the rills are dry, the grass blades are their channels, and from year to year the herds drink at this perennial green stream, and the mower draws from it betimes their winter supply. So our human life but dies down to its root, and still puts forth its green blade to eternity.

• • •

Thanks in Old Age

Thanks in old age — thanks ere I go,
For health, the midday sun, the impalpable
   air — for life, mere life,
For precious ever-lingering memories,
   (of you my mother dear — you,
   father — you, brothers, sisters, friends,)
For all my days — not those of peace alone —
   the days of war the same,
For gentle words, caresses, gifts from
   foreign lands,
For shelter, wine and meat — for sweet
   appreciation,
(You distant, dim unknown — or young or
   old — countless,
   unspecified, readers belov'd,
We never met, and ne'er shall meet — and
   yet our souls embrace, long,
   close and long;)
For beings, groups, love, deeds, words,
   books — for colors, forms,
For all the brave strong men — devoted,
   hardy men —
   who've forward sprung in freedom's help,
   all years, all lands,

For braver, stronger, more devoted men —
    (a special laurel ere I go, to life's war's
    chosen ones,
The cannoneers of song and thought — the
    great artillerists — the foremost leaders,
    captains of the soul:)
As soldier from an ended war return'd — As
    traveler out of myriads, to the long
    procession retrospective,
Thanks — joyful thanks! — a soldier's,
    traveler's thanks.

                 — *Walt Whitman*

A Boy's Town: William Dean Howells

Almost every novelist, sooner or later, tries to recapture in words the world of his youth. In this selection, one of the great novelists of the turn of the century, who grew up in Hamilton, Ohio, presents a vignette of his life, his home and his friends in that town as seen through the eyes of a boy.

Every house, whether it had a flower garden or not, had a woodshed, which was the place where a boy mostly received his friends, and made his kites and wagons, and laid his plots and plans for all the failures of his life. The other boys waited in the woodshed when he went in to ask his mother whether he might do this or that, or go somewhere. A boy always wanted to have a stove in the woodshed and fix it up for himself, but his mother would not let him, because he would have been certain to set the house on fire.

Each fellow knew the inside of his own house tolerably well, but seldom the inside of another fellow's house, and he knew the back yard better than the front yard. If he entered the house of a friend at all, it was to wait for him by the kitchen door, or to get up to the garret with him by the kitchen stairs. If he sometimes, and by some rare mischance, found himself in the living-rooms, or the parlor, he was very unhappy, and anxious to get out. Yet those interiors were not of an oppressive grandeur, and one was much like another. The parlor had what was called a flowered-carpet or gay pattern of ingrain on its floor, and the other rooms had rag-carpets, woven by some woman who had a loom for the work, and dyed at home with such native tints as butternut and foreign colors as logwood. The rooms were all heated with fireplaces, where wood was burned, and coal was never seen. They were lit at night with tallow-candles, which were mostly made by the housewife herself, or by lard-oil glass lamps. In the winter the oil would get so stiff with the cold that it had to be thawed out at the fire before the lamp would burn. There was no such thing as a hot-air furnace known; and the fire on the hearth was kept over from day to day all winter long, by covering a log at night with ashes; in the morning it would be a bed of coals. There were no fires in bedrooms, or at least not in a boy's bedroom, and sometimes he had to break the ice in his pitcher before he could wash; it did not take him very long to dress.

· · ·

The great use of life is to spend it for something that outlasts it.
                    — *William James*

There are two ways of spreading light:
    to be the candle
        or the mirror that reflects it.
                    — *Edith Wharton*

Prayer is the contemplation of the facts of life from the highest point of view.
                    — *Ralph Waldo Emerson*

To see a World in a grain of sand,
    And a Heaven in a wild flower,
Hold Infinity in the palm of your hand,
    And Eternity in an hour.
                    — *William Blake*

Great Spirit, help me never to judge another until I have walked in his moccasins.
                    — *Sioux Indian Prayer*

Diagnosis

On his eightieth birthday, John Quincy Adams responded to a query concerning his well-being by saying: "John Quincy Adams is well. But the house in which he lives at present is becoming dilapidated. It is tottering upon its foundation. Time and the seasons have nearly destroyed it. Its roof is pretty well worn out. Its walls are much shattered and it trembles with every wind. I think John Quincy Adams will have to move out of it soon. But he himself is quite well, quite well."

On Going to Bed: Christopher Morley

Going to bed is one of those human inevitabilities that can be denied by neither the young nor the old, the humble nor the mighty. With a fine touch of whimsy, Mr. Morley explains the nature of this curious reluctance "to hit the hay."

It is a sad thing that as soon as the hands of the clock have turned ten the shadow of going to bed begins to creep over the evening. We have never heard bedtime spoken of with any enthusiasm. One after another we have seen a gathering disperse, each person saying (with an air of solemn resignation): "Well, I guess I'll go to bed." But there was no hilarity about it. It is really rather touching how they cling to the departing skirts of the day that is vanishing under the spinning shadow of night.

This is odd, we repeat, for sleep is highly popular among human beings. The reluctance to go to one's couch is not at all a reluctance to slumber, for almost all of us will doze happily in an armchair or on a sofa, or even festooned on the floor with a couple of cushions. But the actual and formal yielding to sheets and blankets is to be postponed to the last possible moment.

The devil of drowsiness is at his most potent, we find, about 10:30 P.M. At this period the human carcass seems to consider that it has finished its cycle, which began with so much courage nearly sixteen hours before. It begins to slack and the mind halts on a dead centre every now and then, refusing to complete the revolution. Now there are those who hold that this is certainly the seemly and appointed time to go to bed and they do so as a matter of routine. These are, commonly, the happier creatures, for they take the tide of sleep at the flood and are borne calmly and with gracious gentleness out to great waters of nothingness. They push off from the wharf on a tranquil current and nothing more is to be seen or heard of these voyagers until they reappear at the breakfast table, digging lustily into their grape fruit.

These people are happy, aye, in a brutish and sedentary fashion, but they miss the admirable adventures of those more embittered wrestlers who will not give in without a struggle. These latter suffer severe pangs between 10:30 and about 11:15 while they grapple with their fading faculties and seek to reestablish the will on its tottering throne. This requires courage stout, valour unbending. Once you yield, be it ever so little, to the tempter, you are lost. And here our poor barren clay plays us false, undermining the intellect with many a trick and wile. "I will sit down for a season in that comfortable chair," the creature says to himself, "and read this sprightly novel. That will ease my mind and put me in humour for a continuance of lively thinking." And the end of that man is a steady nasal buzz from the bottom of the chair where he has collapsed, an unsightly object and a disgrace to humanity.

• • •

The Coin

Into my heart's treasury
   I slipped a coin,
That time cannot rust
   Nor a thief purloin;
Oh, better than the minting
   Of a gold-crowned king
Is the safe-kept memory
   Of a lovely thing.
        — *Sara Teasdale*

A New Style of Aging:
Margaret Mead

America's widely known anthropologist explains the valuable contribution the elderly can make if they will assert themselves and if society, in turn, will open its doors to them.

On the subways I've been riding for fifty years, two things have happened: people have stopped giving up their seats to the old, and old people have stopped accepting seats when they are offered. "I'll stand, thank you."

What we need to do is to find a style of aging that will keep and foster this independence, but will encourage old people to think in terms of what they can do for someone else. If we are going to change the style, the relationship between young and old, older people will have to take the lead by finding ways to relate either to their own grandchildren or to someone else's.

As long as we say that youth has no need for age, that young people in this country aren't interested in old people, in seeing them or listening to them, there will be an enormous number of things in our society that are not being done, but which could be done, by old people. It is true that it is very hard to get employment if you look the least bit old. But there are many things to be done in society that don't have to be done under the auspices of employment agencies.

What we need in this society more than anything else is warm bodies who can sit by a door, answer a telephone, stay around until the plumber comes. There are masses of people sitting around being independent and keeping healthy who could be sitting in somebody's house freeing that person to get out and go to work.

We are beginning to think about day care centers and we ought to bring older people in. PTA's should encourage older people to participate, *not* throw out the mothers the minute their last children leave the school....

This country is filled with widows who sit around in eight-room houses polishing furniture instead of being of any use to the world. They'll tell you that nobody wants them, that nobody listens to old people anymore, but it isn't true. Or it's only as true as they make it true.

There isn't any reason society shouldn't be reorganized along new lines by finding places where old people are really useful. Old people themselves have to begin asking the question, "Where and how can I continue to make a contribution?"...

There are a thousand ways old people can contribute if we only set up the housing, the neighborhoods, the living arrangements that make it feasible for them to do so.

• • •

The hands of those I meet are dumbly eloquent to me. The touch of some hands is an impertinence. I have met people so empty of joy that when I clasped their frosty fingertips it seemed as if I were shaking hands with a northeast storm. Others there are whose hands have sunbeams in them, so that their grasp warms my heart.

— *Helen Keller*

Life is no brief candle to me. It is a sort of splendid torch which I have got hold of for the moment, and I want to make it burn as brightly as possible before handing it on to future generations.

— *George Bernard Shaw*

Toward Greater Vitality:
Justice William O. Douglas

The word "vitality" is probably the single word that most accurately characterizes U.S. Supreme Court Justice Douglas, a man of great creative energy at age seventy-four. And in the view of Justice Douglas, vitality is the central element of a creative life.

In my own life challenge has played an important role. For years I had a deep-seated competitive drive that was motivated by crippling polio, which cost me the use of my legs from the time I was four until I was six. The desire to walk, to run, to walk thousands of miles was a burning force in my life. It led me first to the foothills outside the town of Yakima, Washington, where I grew up, then to the mountains, and finally to the great Himalayas, where, at the age of fifty-three, I reached 22,000 feet without the use of oxygen.

Vitality, in many cases, is a response to challenges met and overcome. Put another way, vitality thrives on challenge, provided there is hope. The political prisoner in a miserable camp remains alive and vital by the knowledge that the conscience of men will in time respond to his distress. The crippled child has the challenge to walk — and his hope is in reaching the top of a mountain to see over and beyond it.

Surely the word *vitality* has meaning only through vital people, past and present. If there is something in common among all such men and women, it is that they give their lives to something larger than self. History values most that something — whether it's an art, a science, or a cause. Surely this quality, or gift, is very close to what we call creativity as well.

In my seventy-four years I've been privileged to know many men and women with this great gift for life; and I have been inspired by many others both past and present.

This creative immersion in life can take many forms. It certainly does not require sophistication or even great experience in the world. Zoroaster, Confucius, Moses, Buddha, Christ, Mohammed, and Joseph Smith were provincial in the sense that they knew only their immediate neighborhood. But they were inspired by the spiritual needs of those people who lived next door. Sensing what those needs were, they put into creed, dogma, and moral codes principles that guided men over the centuries, no matter what the color of their skin or the language they spoke. The vitality of such men led to creative philosophies that ordered the activities of entire societies.

• • •

I find the great thing in this world is not so much where we stand, as *in what direction we are moving.* To reach the port of heaven, we must sail sometimes with the wind, and sometimes against it; but we must sail, and not drift, nor lie at anchor.

— *Oliver Wendell Holmes*

When I was a boy of fourteen, my father was so ignorant I could hardly stand to have the old man around. But when I got to be twenty-one, I was astonished at how much the old man had learned in seven years.

— *Mark Twain*

To be popular at home is a great achievement. The man who is loved by the house cat, by the dog, by the neighbor's children, and by his own wife, is a great man, even if he has never had his name in *Who's Who*.

— *Thomas Dreier*

No man is an island, entire of itself; every man is a piece of the continent, a part of the main. If a clod be washed away by the sea, Europe is the less, as well as if a promontory were, as well as if a manor of thy friend's or of thine own were: any man's death diminishes me, because I am involved in mankind, and therefore never send to know for whom the bell tolls; it tolls for thee.

— *John Donne*

Journey in a Circle: John P. Marquand

Mr. Marquand traveled extensively in his lifetime — Europe, the Middle East, Southeast Asia and China. But no matter how far he went, he learned "the road one takes...always turns toward home."

It becomes plainer to me every year that there can be no promised land except the land within one's mind, and that is apt to be a shifting, unsatisfactory region. My own road has always turned toward home. My thoughts continually return to the place where my ancestors have come from and where I spent most of my childhood. It is a seaport town in Massachusetts with many disadvantages and many limitations. It has no great beauty nor great sources of stimulation but it has the great advantage of being a place where I belong, and probably this definite feeling of belonging is what makes it desirable. What is more, it is inescapable, the memory of an austere church spire and elm trees and of a cold sea and salt marshes has been with me during all my travels. In a way it has been the one reality, since it has been the only place where I have ever really lived and the only place from which I have ever tried earnestly and wholeheartedly to escape. I have tried to get its provincial accent from my speech and its conscientious narrowness from my mind. The difficulties I have had with that early environment, the youthful revolt I have experienced against it have in the end only made me respect its memories. For me, and I am willing to wager for everyone else, the road one takes, no matter how far it goes, always leads to a contradictory sort of frustration, because it always leads to accidental beginnings. It always turns toward home.

• • •

If we are ever to enjoy life, *now* is the time — not tomorrow, nor next year, nor in some future life after we have died.

The best preparation for a better life next year is a full, complete, harmonious, joyous life this year.

Our beliefs in a rich future life are of little importance unless we coin them into a rich present life.

Today should always be our most wonderful day!

— *Thomas Dreier*

The Zest of Life

Let me but live from year to year,
    With forward face and unreluctant soul;
    Not hurrying to, nor turning from,
        the goal;
Not mourning for the things that disappear
In the dim past, nor holding back in fear
    From what the future veils; but with
        a whole
    And happy heart, that pays its toll
To Youth and Age, and travels on with cheer.
So let the way wind up the hill or down
    O'er rough or smooth, the journey will
        be joy:
    Still seeking what I sought when but
        a boy,
New friendship, high adventure, and
        a crown,
    My heart will keep the courage of
        the quest,
    And hope the road's last turn will be
        the best.

— Henry van Dyke

A Fine Old Man

John Wagner, the oldest man in Buffalo — one hundred and four years old — recently walked a mile and a half in two weeks.

He is as cheerful and bright as any of these other old men that charge around so persistently and tiresomely in the newspapers, and in every way as remarkable.

Last November he walked five blocks in a rainstorm, without any shelter but an umbrella, and cast his vote for Grant, remarking that he had voted for forty-seven presidents — which was a lie.

His "second crop" of rich brown hair arrived from New York yesterday, and he has a new set of teeth coming — from Philadelphia.

He is to be married next week to a girl one hundred and two years old, who still takes in washing.

They have been engaged eighty years, but their parents persistently refused their consent until three days ago.

John Wagner is two years older than the Rhode Island veteran, and yet has never tasted a drop of liquor in his life — unless — unless you count whisky.

— Mark Twain

Set in Trump Medieval, a Venetian face
designed by Professor Georg Trump, in Munich.
Printed on Hallmark Eggshell Book paper.